A HOUSE OF PRAYER

An excerpt from Teach Us to Pray

And he says to them, It is written,
My house shall be called a house of prayer.
—Matthew 21:13

A HOUSE OF PRAYER

An excerpt from *Teach Us to Pray*

Stephen Kaung

Christian Fellowship Publishers, Inc.
New York

Paperback ISBN: 978-1-68062-189-1
eBook ISBN: 978-1-68062-190-7

Available from the Publishers at:

11515 Allecingie Parkway
Richmond, Virginia 23235
www.c-f-p.com

Printed in the United States of America

Note

This brief sharing on *A House of Prayer* was originally published as chapter 11 in the book *Teach Us to Pray*, also available from Christian Fellowship Publishers.

Unless otherwise indicated,
Scripture quotations are from the
New Translation by J. N. Darby.

A House of Prayer

II Chronicles 6:18-21, 40-42—But will God indeed dwell with man on the earth? behold, the heavens and the heaven of heavens cannot contain thee; how much less this house which I have built! Yet have respect unto the prayer of thy servant, and to his supplication, Jehovah, my God, to hearken unto the cry and to the prayer which thy servant prayeth before thee; that thine eyes may be open upon this house day and night, upon the place in which thou hast said thou wouldest put thy name: to hearken unto the prayer which thy servant prayeth toward this place. And hearken unto the supplications of thy servant, and of thy people Israel, which they shall pray toward this place, and hear thou from thy dwelling-place, from the heavens, and when thou hearest, forgive.

II Chronicles 6:40-42—Now, my God, I beseech thee, let thine eyes be open and let thine ears be attentive unto the prayer that is made in this place. And now, arise, Jehovah Elohim, into thy resting-place, thou and the ark of thy strength: let thy priests, Jehovah Elohim, be clothed with salvation, and let thy saints rejoice in thy goodness. Jehovah Elohim, turn not away the face of thine anointed: remember mercies to David thy servant.

Matthew 21:13—… It is written, My house shall be called a house of prayer.

Solomon built the temple, and when it was dedicated, he acknowledged that God really did not dwell in a physical house because even "the heavens and the heaven of heavens cannot contain thee; how much less this house which I have built!" Even though it was a magnificent building, he understood that God did not actually dwell there; yet, it was where God put His name. Because His name was there, Solomon expected God to hear all the prayers that would be offered in the temple and even those prayers that were offered towards it.

In II Chronicles 6, Solomon raised up all kinds of imaginable situations such as being attacked by the enemy, famine, war, pestilence, plagues, people sinning, or taking an oath. He said whatever the situation might be—whether the people there repented and prayed in the temple, or if they had been taken to the corners of the earth and prayed towards the temple—God would hear, forgive, deliver, and answer.

When our Lord Jesus was on earth, He said, "Is it not written, My house shall be called a house of prayer for all the nations?" (Mark 11:17) So the temple was actually a house of prayer for all nations. It was not only for the children of Israel, but even if strangers should turn towards the temple and pray, God would hear. Can you imagine the temple standing there and no prayers being offered in it or towards it? It is impossible.

Under the New Covenant, we are the temple of God. In Ephesians 2, it is stated very clearly:

> Being built upon the foundation of the apostles and prophets, Jesus Christ himself being the corner-stone, in whom all the building fitted together increases to a holy temple in the Lord; in whom ye also are built together for a habitation of God in the Spirit (vv. 20-22).

Today the Lord is building a temple with living stones. He is building us together to be the house of God.

In this house, you will find not only His name but also His presence. In Matthew 18, He said,

> For where two or three are gathered together unto my name, there am I in the midst of them (v. 20).

Today, God is actually dwelling in this house. He did not do that with the temple built by Solomon, but He does dwell in this temple built with living stones. He said, "There am I in the midst of them." He makes His residence in the church. Therefore, today, how much more real is the church as the house of prayer for all nations.

The church is called to pray, and we will find this was true at the beginning of church history, as recorded in the book of Acts:

> And they persevered in the teaching and fellowship of the apostles, in breaking of bread and prayers (2:42).

Whenever anything has happened, the church has turned to prayer. It is a praying church; it is a house of prayer. The ministry of the church is basically prayer, but unfortunately, today people seem to flock to the time when the word is ministered. Thank God for that. People love to hear the Word, but when it comes to the time of prayer, many people disappear.

And in some places, there is no prayer meeting because people will not come to pray. If that is the case, it shows whether there is a church or not. If there is a church, there should be prayer. Unless we come to an understanding of what prayer is, we do not know what the church is. Or, to put it in another way, we never really enter into the life of the church. It is a very serious thing to come to a meeting of prayer. If we do not see the importance of coming together to pray, then actually, we do not know what the church is, and we do not practice church life. People who come together to pray are those who are really appreciating, appropriating, and living church life.

In the Old Testament, when the priests served in the temple offering incense at the golden altar of incense, this was the highest service they could ever perform.

We are told that at the time of Christ, a lot could fall upon a certain priest to offer incense at the golden altar of incense. He could do this only once in his lifetime. It could never be repeated. Many priests served during their entire lives in the temple and were never given this privilege by God.

Today we are not only the house of God; we are also the priesthood serving in the house of God. Everyone has the privilege to burn incense at the golden altar of incense—not just once, but it is a lifetime job. We can do it all the time.

Furthermore, in the Old Testament times, when the priests burned incense, there was a veil separating the altar of incense from the mercy seat; but today, the veil is rent. When we pray, we enter into the very presence of God with unveiled face—face to face. There we can offer prayers on behalf of God's people, for the world, for God's interest, His kingdom, and His concern. Every imaginable situation can be brought before the Lord in prayer. That is our calling, our privilege, and our right. I do hope we appreciate this.

Suppose we were living thousands of years ago as priests in the temple built by Solomon or rebuilt by the remnant. We would long to burn incense at the golden altar of incense, but more than likely, we would not have the opportunity. However, in our day, it is a privilege and a right that is ours. Can you even imagine that we are not exercising our right and appreciating our privilege to burn incense at the golden altar of incense?

If we could only know what this means, we would appreciate the time when the church gathers together to pray. We know that when we pray, He is listening; His eyes are open; His ears are open; His heart is open;

His name is here; His presence is here. How much He will forgive, deliver, and answer.

May we appreciate this time when we come together.

Titles Available by Stephen Kaung

Abiding in God
Acts: the Working of the Holy Spirit
A Man in Christ
— *Traditional Chinese Version*
— *Simplified Chinese Version*
"But We See Jesus":
The Life of the Lord Jesus
The Charge to the Church:
How Will The Church Be Made Right?
Concerning Spirituals – Vol. 1:
Vision, Responsibility, Ministry
Concerning Spirituals – Vol. 2:
Authority, House, Submission
David: Characteristics of a Spiritual Leader
Discipled to Christ:
As Seen in the Life of Simon Peter
Elijah and Elisha: One Prophetic Ministry
Glory: As Seen by Ezekiel
God's Purpose for the Family
Government and Ministry in the Church
The Gymnasium of Christ

Haggai
In the Footsteps of Christ
I Corinthians: Called into Fellowship
II Corinthians: A Man in Christ
Isaiah: the Redemption of the Lord
The Key to "Revelation" – Vol. 1
The Key to "Revelation" – Vol. 2
Malachi
— *English Version*
— *Traditional Chinese Version*
— *Simplified Chinese Version*
The Master's Training
Men After God's Own Heart
Ministering the Word of God
Moses, the Servant of God
Nehemiah: Recovering the Testimony of God
New Covenant Living & Ministry
Now We See the Church:
the Life of the Church, the Body of Christ
Proverbs: Wisdom Builds God's House
Recovery
Seven Visions of Christ in the Book of Revelation
Shepherding

Teach Us to Pray
The Songs of Degrees: Meditations on Fifteen Psalms
The Sons of Korah
The Splendor of His Ways:
Seeing the Lord's End in Job
Titus
Worship
Zechariah

<u>The "God Has Spoken" Series</u>
Seeing Christ in the Old Testament, Part One
Seeing Christ in the Old Testament, Part Two
Seeing Christ in the New Testament